ETA COHEN'S
YOUNG
RECITAL PIECES

BOOK 1

Enjoyable repertoire for young violinists

Novello Publishing Limited
8-9 Frith Street, London W1V 5TZ

Exclusive distributors:
Music Sales Limited
Newmarket Road, Bury St Edmunds,
Suffolk IP33 3YB.
All rights reserved.

Order No. NOV916180
ISBN 0-85360-559-9
© Copyright 1996 Novello & Company Limited.
8/9 Frith Street, London W1V 5TZ.

Music set by Stave Origination.
Cover design by Xheight Limited.
Printed in the United Kingdom by
Caligraving Limited, Thetford, Norfolk.

CONTENTS

SUITE OF TEN PIECES

1 Siesta

Use full straight bows for every note.
Try to play half-way between the bridge and fingerboard,
but move nearer the bridge when playing *mf* or *f*.
This piece should be very calm.

VIOLIN

Christine Brown

2 On Parade

Play this with strong rhythm and keep it very lively.
Use whole bows for the minims,
half bows for the crotchets
and very short bows for the quavers.

Christine Brown

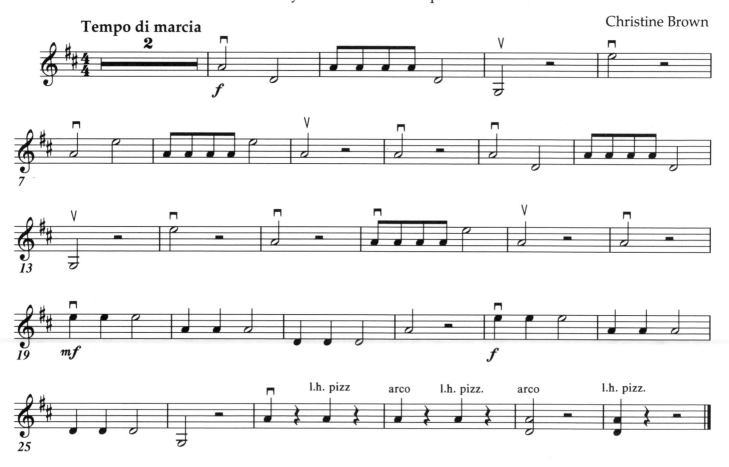

3 The Skaters

Try to imagine you are skating on ice!
Use whole bows in every bar.

Christine Brown

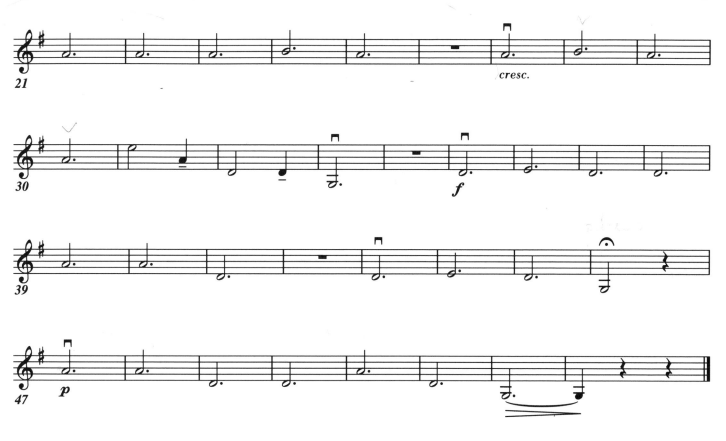

4 Bye, Bye, Baby

This is useful for practising playing on the G string - remember to
hold your arm fairly high. Play with a gentle rhythm in the style of a lullaby.
Whole bows for crotchets, half bows for quavers and slower whole bows for minims.

(Appalachian Lullaby)
Arr. Christine Brown

5 Unto Us Is Born A Son

Remember to use half bows for crotchets
and whole bows for minims and slurred crotchets.

(Melody from Piae Cantiones, 1582)
Arr. Christine Brown

6 Thistledown

Make sure you use whole bows throughout this piece, but play gently.

Christine Brown

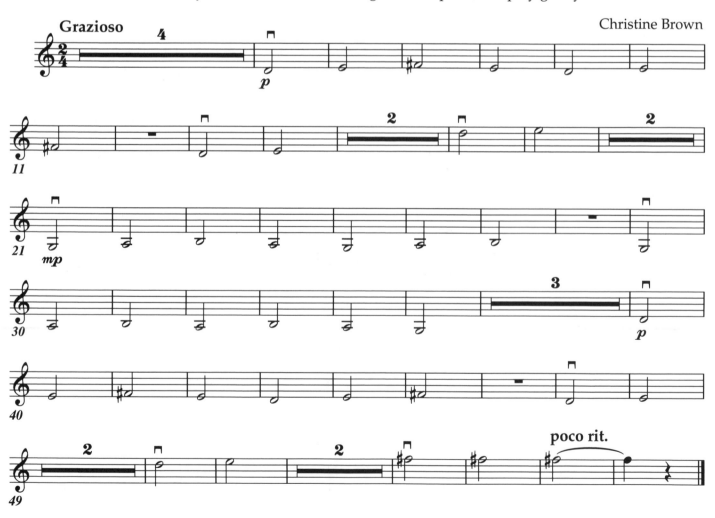

7 Square Dance

Use whole bows from bar 28, but the
middle of the bow for the rest of the piece.
Play energetically, as if to encourage the dancers!

Allegro energico

Christine Brown

8 Lament

Play very slowly, with whole bows throughout.

Andante doloroso

Christine Brown

9 Daydreams

Make sure you use whole bows throughout.
Where you have a tied note, draw the bow very slowly.
Notice the broken slurs.

Christine Brown

10 Fiddle-de-dee

Play the quavers with short bows either at the point or the heel.
Use whole bows for the minims.

Christine Brown

WALTZ

Use whole bows throughout.
Imagine you are accompanying dancers waltzing around the room!

Allegretto

Emma Rivlin

CALLER HERRIN'

Use whole bows for crotchets and slurred quavers,
and short bows for separate quavers.

Traditional
Arr. Hywel Davies

NOW LET US TO THE BAGPIPE SOUND

Play this vigorously!

J.S. Bach
(Cantata BWV 212)
Arr. Hywel Davies

SEE THE CONQUERING HERO COMES

Play triumphantly with very firm bowing
- whole bows for minims, half bows for crotchets
and short bows for quavers.

G.F. Handel
(*from Judas Maccabeus*)
Arr. Hywel Davies

THE IRISH WASHERWOMAN

Use only the middle of the bow.
Be sure to start each bar with a ⊓ and every half bar with a ∨.
Play vigorously!

Traditional
Arr. Hywel Davies

MY LOVE SHE'S BUT A LASSIE YET

Use the middle of the bow.
This piece should sound lighthearted and happy.

Traditional
Arr. Hywel Davies

ETA COHEN'S
YOUNG
RECITAL PIECES
BOOK 1

Enjoyable repertoire for young violinists

Novello Publishing Limited
8-9 Frith Street, London W1V 5TZ

Exclusive distributors:
Music Sales Limited
Newmarket Road, Bury St Edmunds,
Suffolk IP33 3YB.
All rights reserved.

Order No. NOV916180
ISBN 0-85360-559-9
© Copyright 1996 Novello & Company Limited.
8/9 Frith Street, London W1V 5TZ.

Music set by Stave Origination.
Cover design by Xheight Limited.
Printed in the United Kingdom by
Caligraving Limited, Thetford, Norfolk.

CONTENTS

SUITE OF TEN PIECES

1 Siesta

Use full straight bows for every note.
Try to play half-way between the bridge and fingerboard,
but move nearer the bridge when playing *mf* or *f*.
This piece should be very calm.

Christine Brown

All Rights Reserved

3

2 On Parade

Play this with strong rhythm and keep it very lively.
Use whole bows for the minims,
half bows for the crotchets
and very short bows for the quavers.

Christine Brown

3 The Skaters

Try to imagine you are skating on ice!
Use whole bows in every bar.

Christine Brown

4 Bye, Bye, Baby

This is useful for practising playing on the G string - remember to
hold your arm fairly high. Play with a gentle rhythm in the style of a lullaby.
Whole bows for crotchets, half bows for quavers and slower whole bows for minims.

(Appalachian Lullaby)
Arr. Christine Brown

5 Unto Us Is Born A Son

Remember to use half bows for crotchets
and whole bows for minims and slurred crotchets.

(Melody from Piae Cantiones, 1582)
Arr. Christine Brown

6 Thistledown

Make sure you use whole bows throughout this piece, but play gently.

Christine Brown

7 Square Dance

Use whole bows from bar 28, but the
middle of the bow for the rest of the piece.
Play energetically, as if to encourage the dancers!

Christine Brown

8 Lament

Play very slowly, with whole bows throughout.

Christine Brown

9 Daydreams

Make sure you use whole bows throughout.
Where you have a tied note, draw the bow very slowly.
Notice the broken slurs.

Christine Brown

10 Fiddle-de-dee

Play the quavers with short bows either at the point or the heel.
Use whole bows for the minims.

Christine Brown

WALTZ

Use whole bows throughout.
Imagine you are accompanying dancers waltzing around the room!

Emma Rivlin

CALLER HERRIN'

Use whole bows for crotchets and slurred quavers,
and short bows for separate quavers.

Traditional
Arr. Hywel Davies

NOW LET US TO THE BAGPIPE SOUND

Play this vigorously!

J.S. Bach
(Cantata BWV 212)
Arr. Hywel Davies

SEE THE CONQUERING HERO COMES

Play triumphantly with very firm bowing
- whole bows for minims, half bows for crotchets
and short bows for quavers.

G.F. Handel
(from Judas Maccabeus)
Arr. Hywel Davies

THE IRISH WASHERWOMAN

Use only the middle of the bow.
Be sure to start each bar with a ⊓ and every half bar with a ∨.
Play vigorously!

Traditional
Arr. Hywel Davies

MY LOVE SHE'S BUT A LASSIE YET

Use the middle of the bow.
This piece should sound lighthearted and happy.

Traditional
Arr. Hywel Davies